Dear little artists, this coloring book is dedicated to you. May each stroke be an adventure, each color an emotion, and each page a world of imagination. May this book be the beginning of many colorful and fun journeys for you. May your creations bring smiles, inspiration, and a sparkle in your eyes. Here's to you, the bright minds and creative hearts, who make the world a more colorful place with.

Marcella Melo
2024

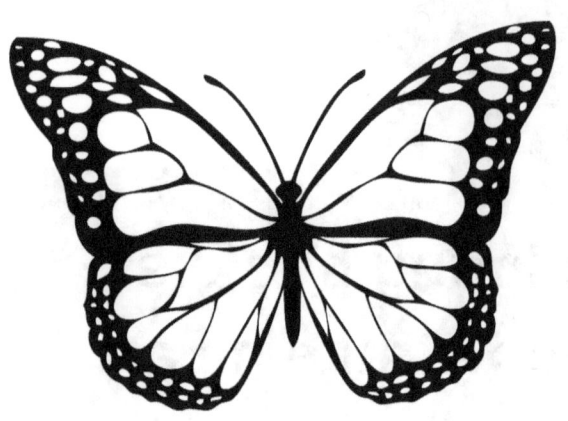
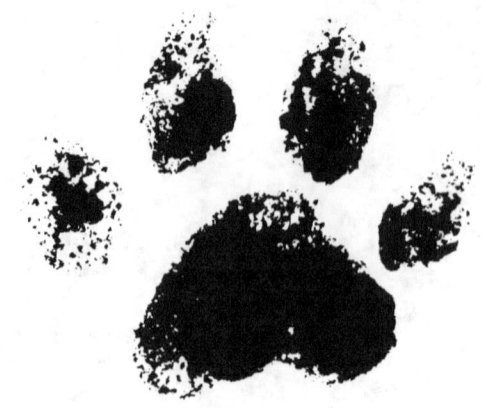

This book belongs to:

_____

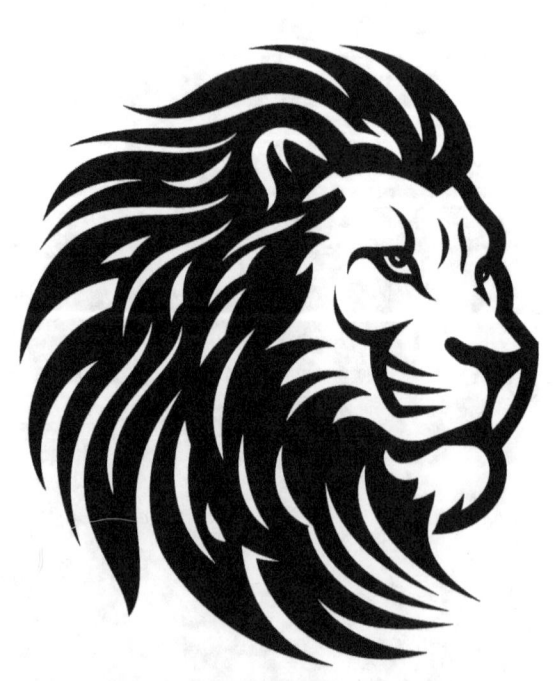
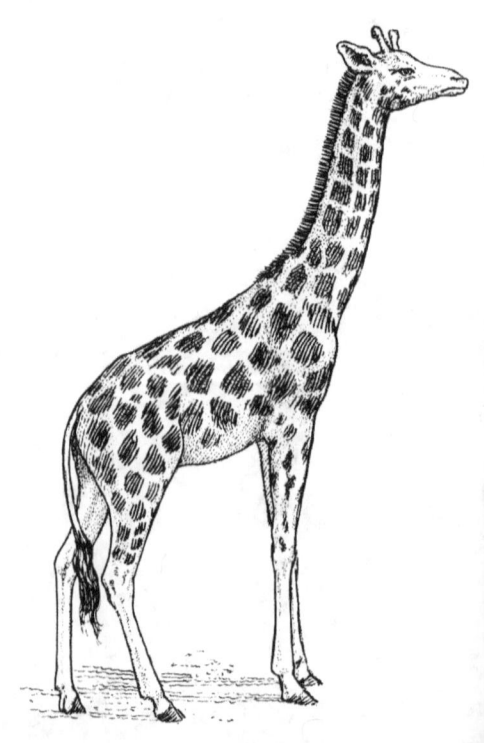

color test table

ALL RIGHTS RESERVED ©
2024

Certainly! Here is a copyright notice for an English coloring book:

All rights reserved. No part of this coloring book may be reproduced, distributed or transmitted in any form or by any means, including photocopying, recording or other electronic or mechanical methods, without the prior written permission of the publisher, except in the case of brief quotations. incorporated in critical reviews and certain other non-commercial uses permitted by copyright law.

Marcellla Melo ©

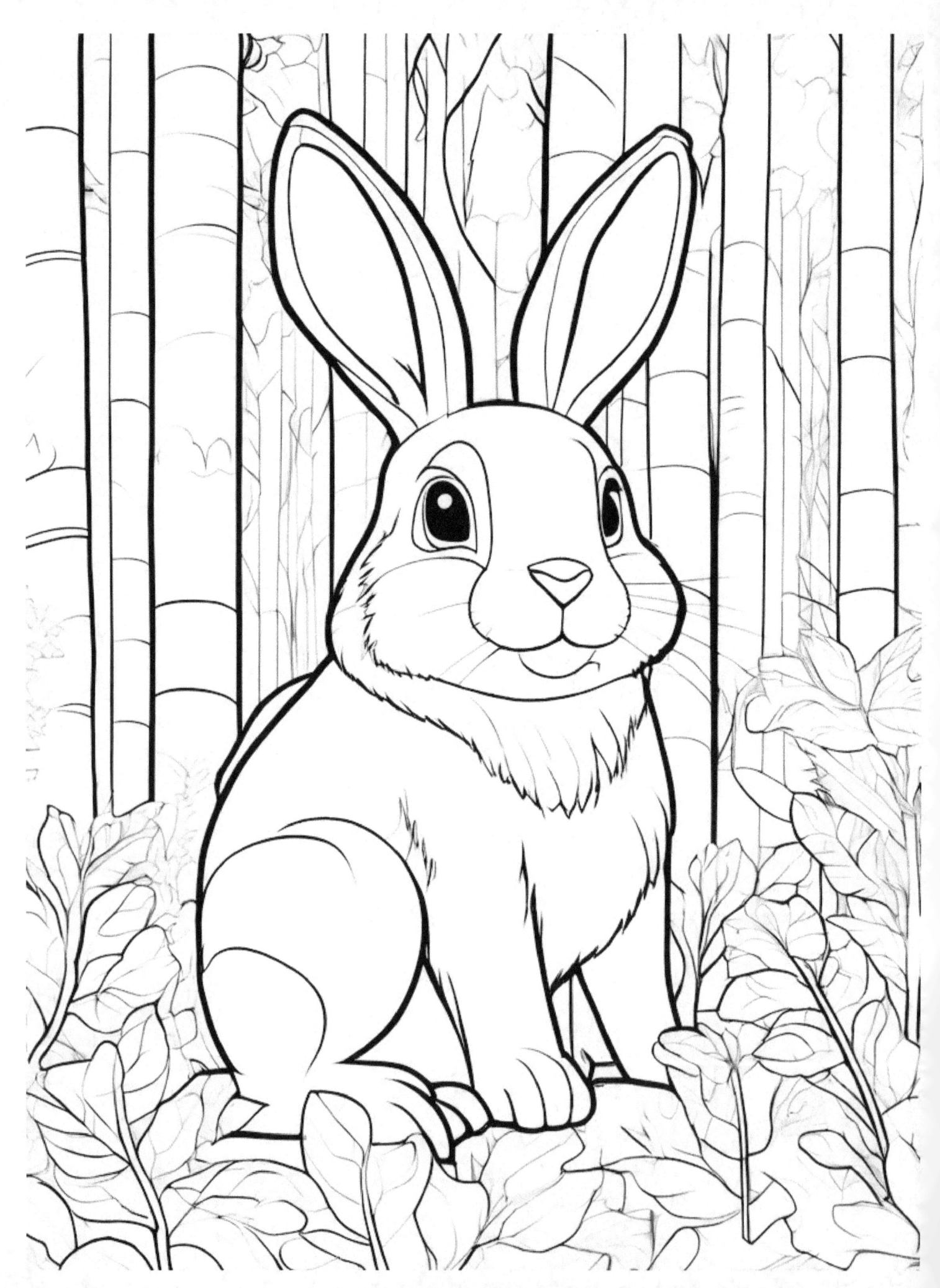

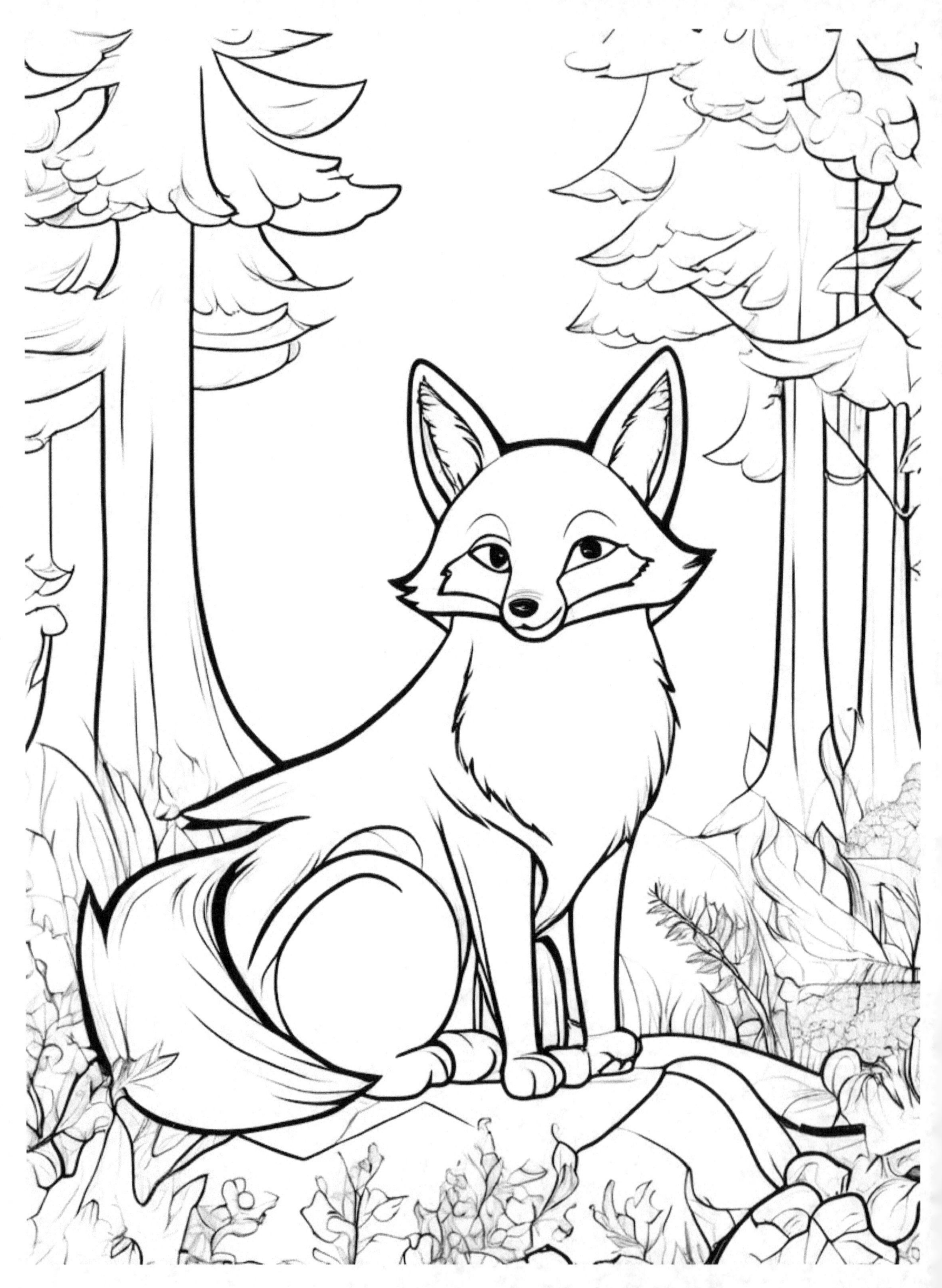

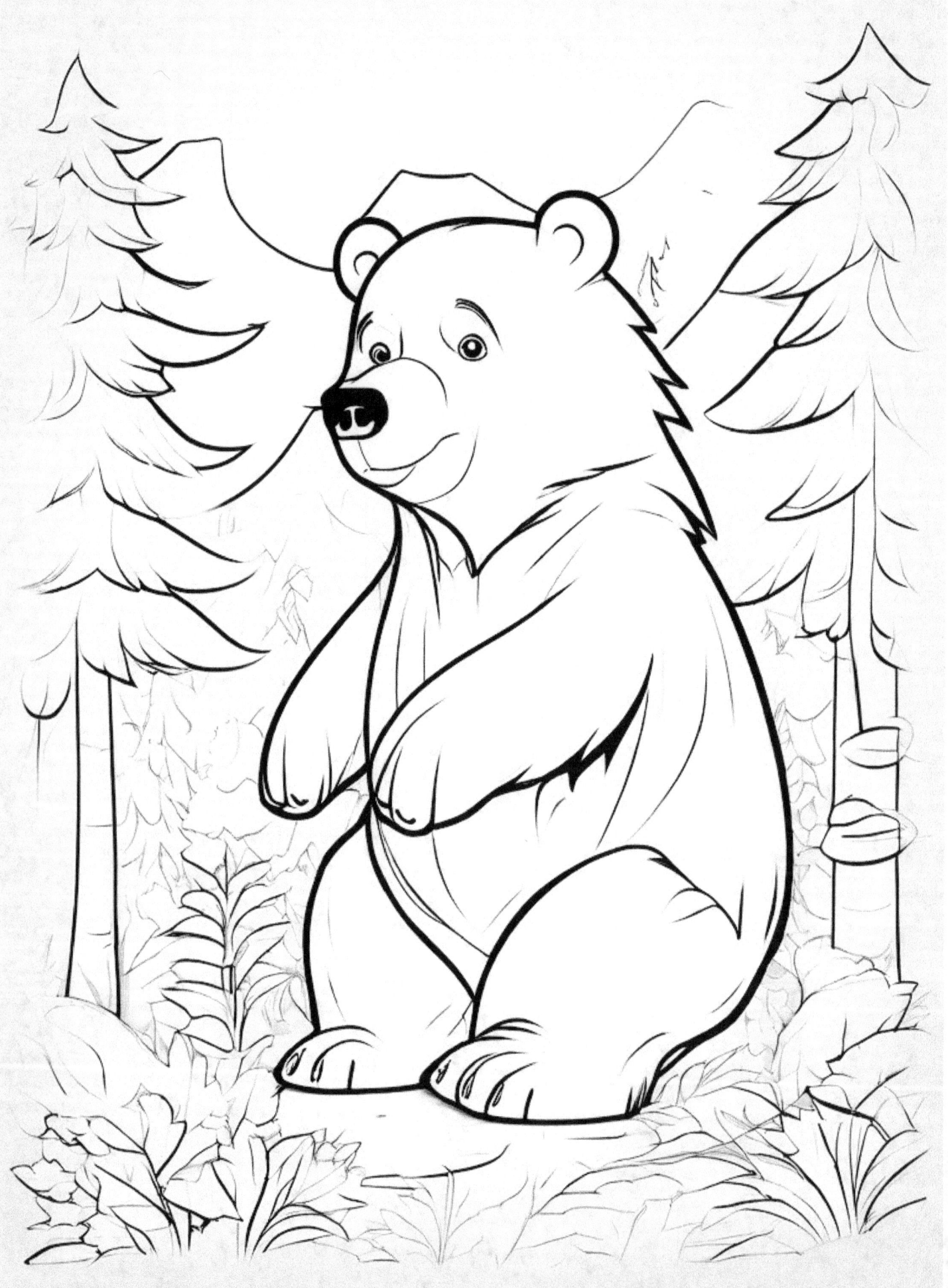

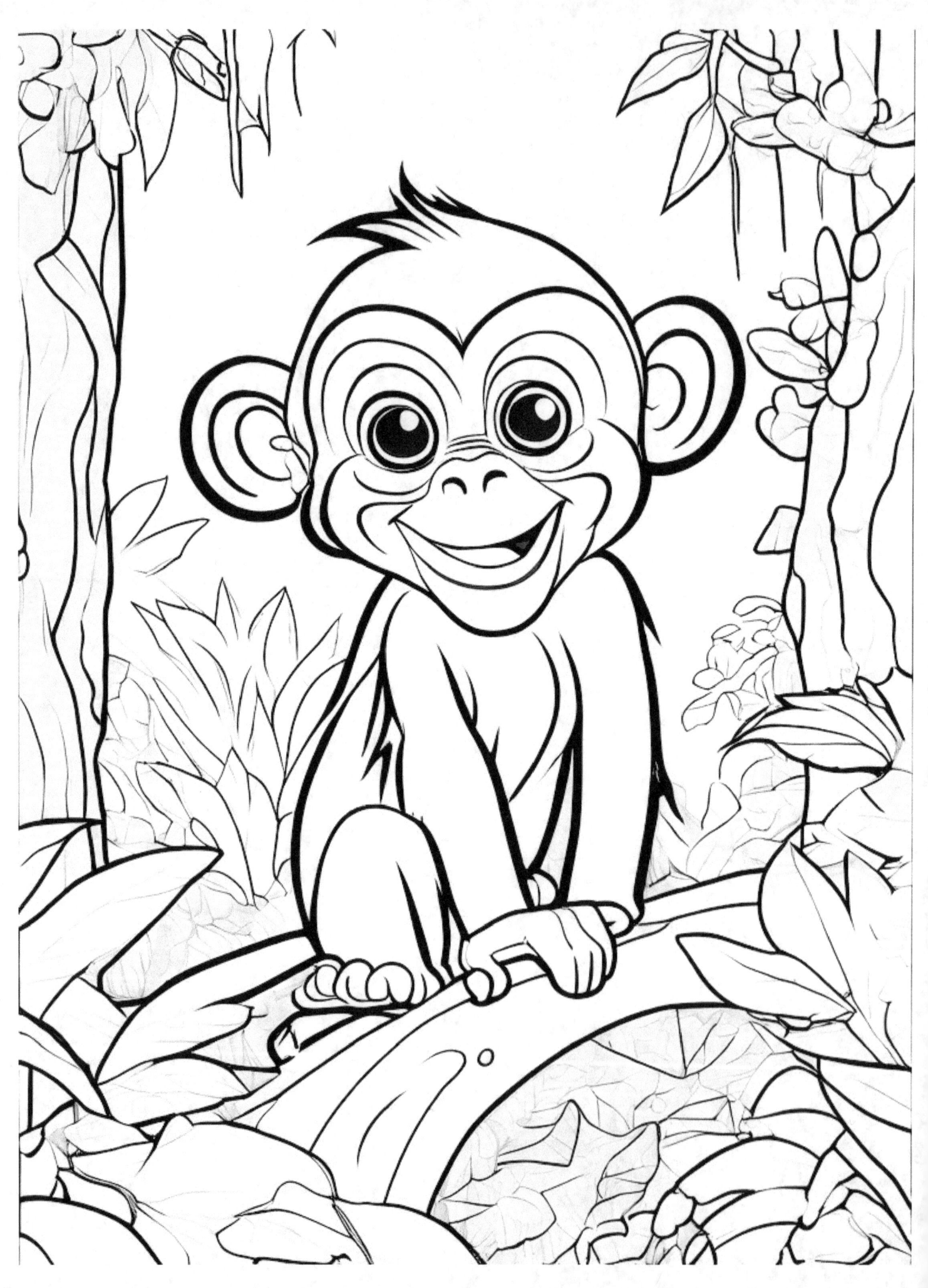

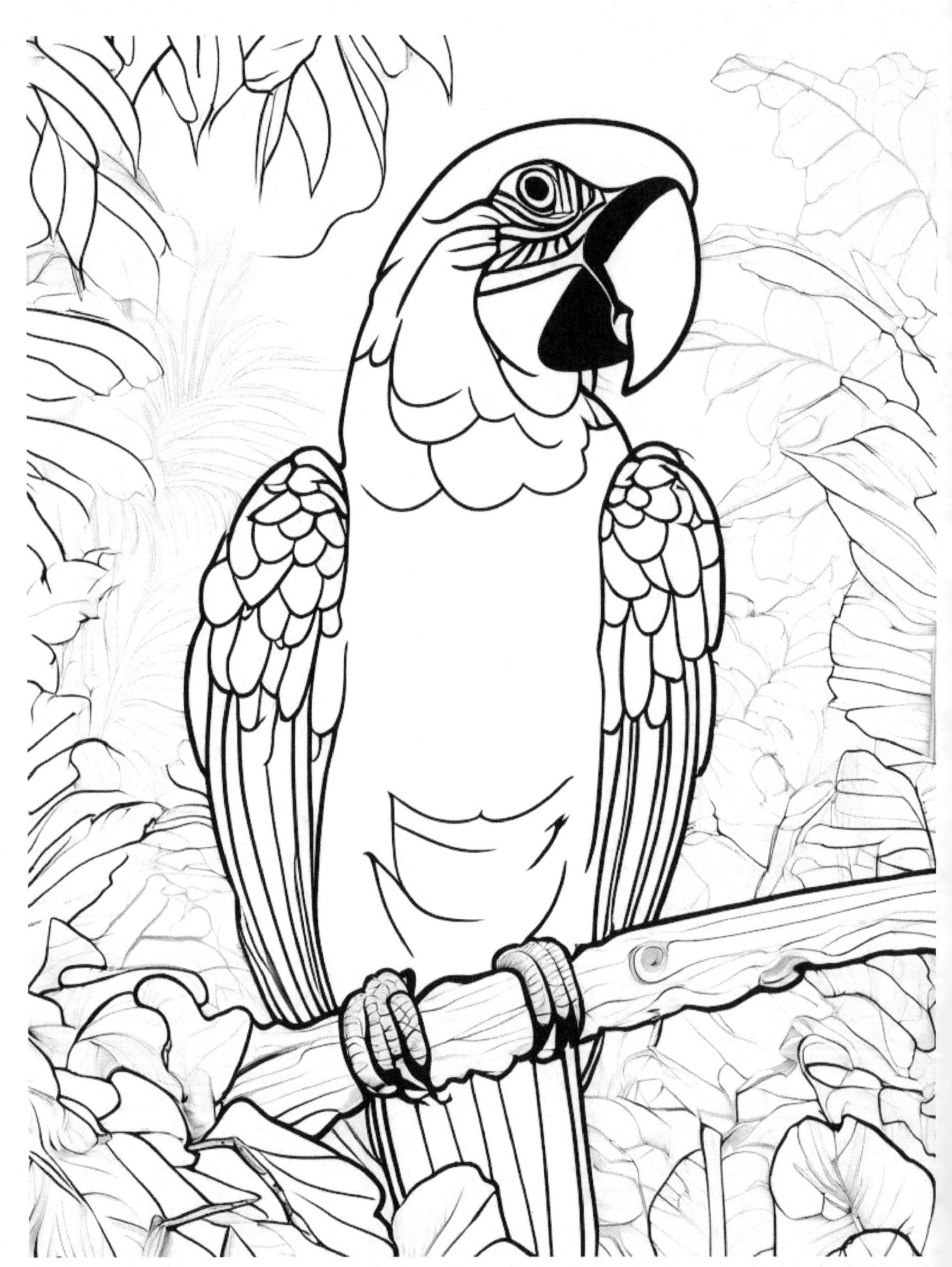

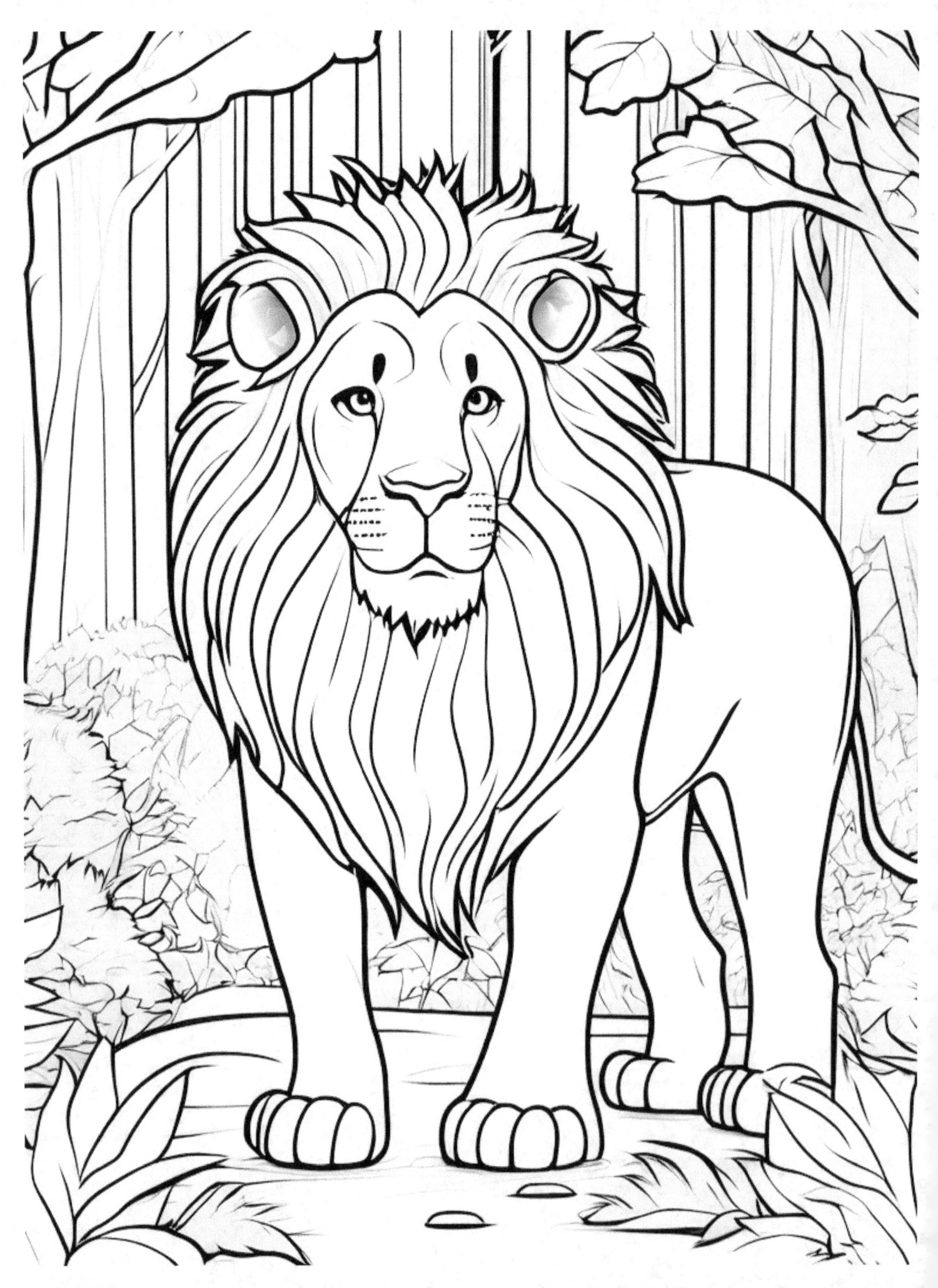

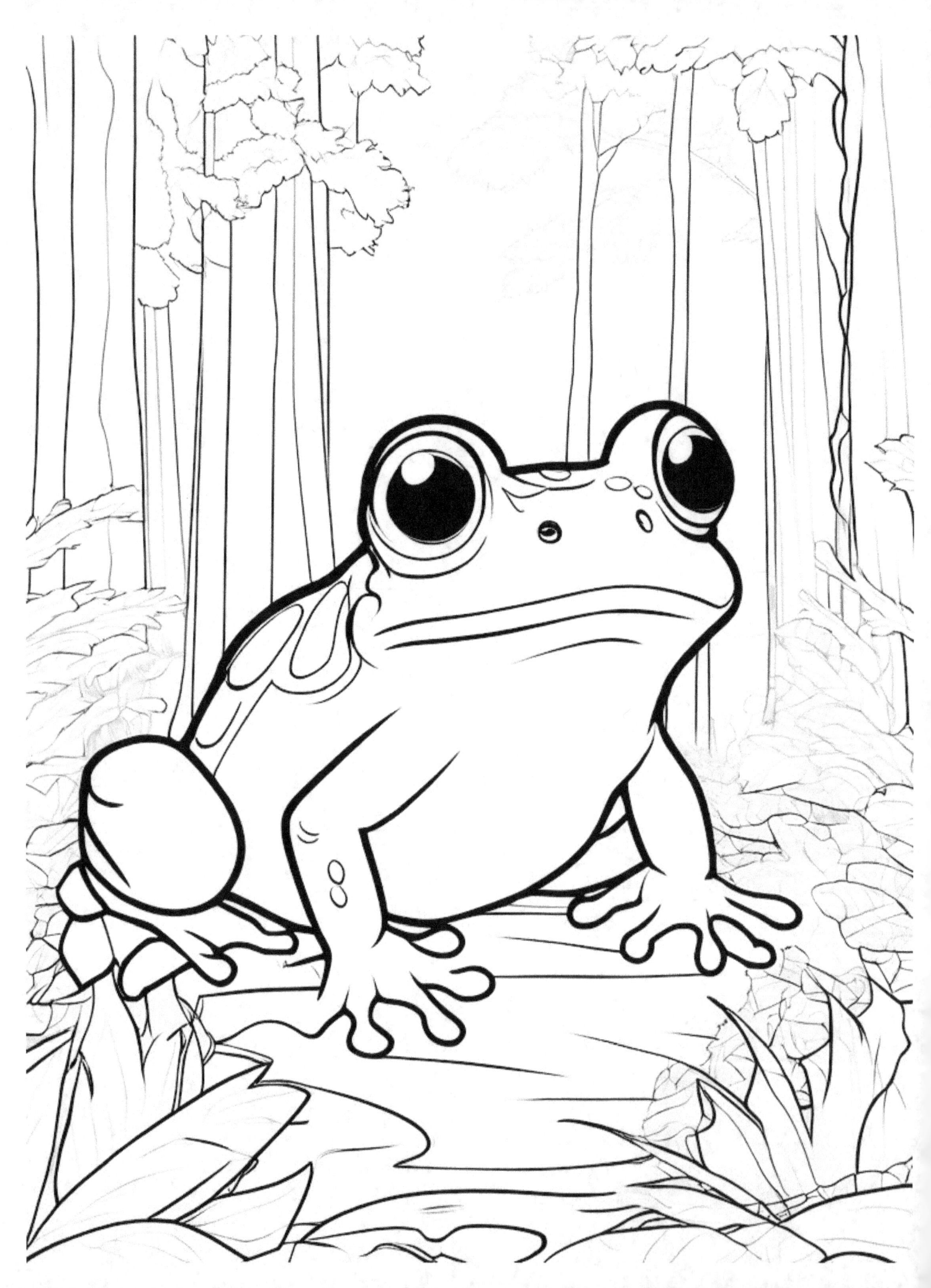

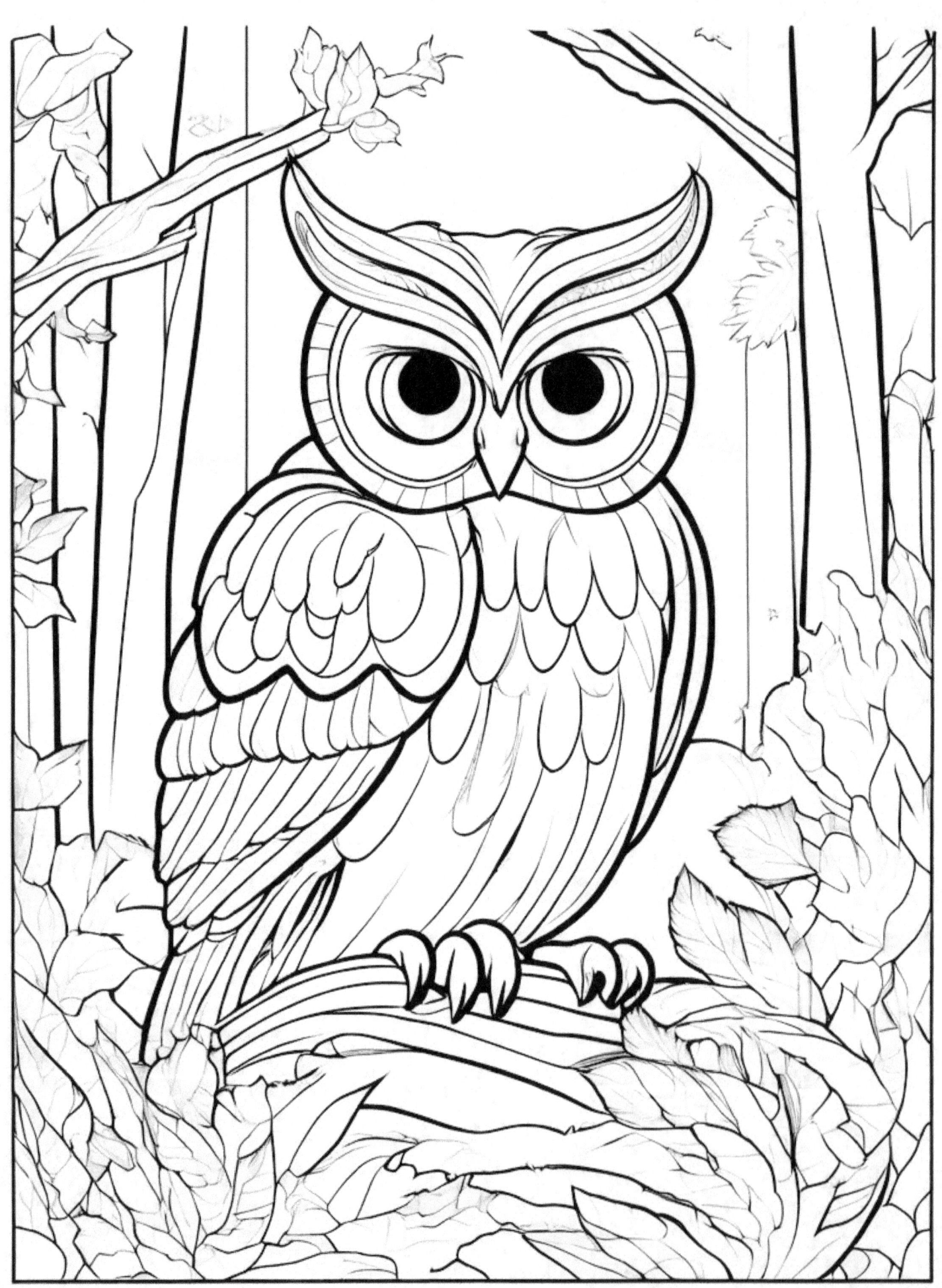

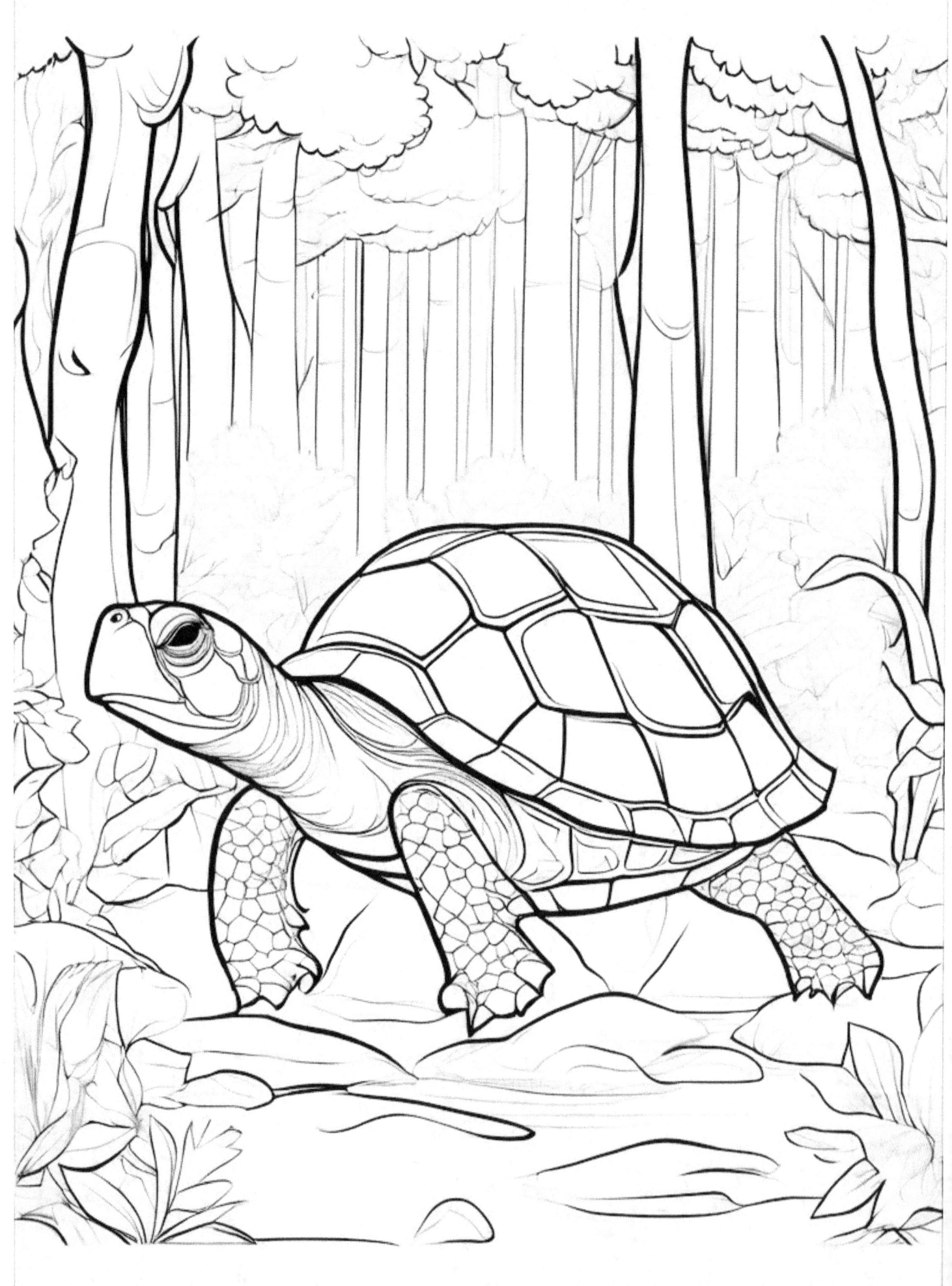

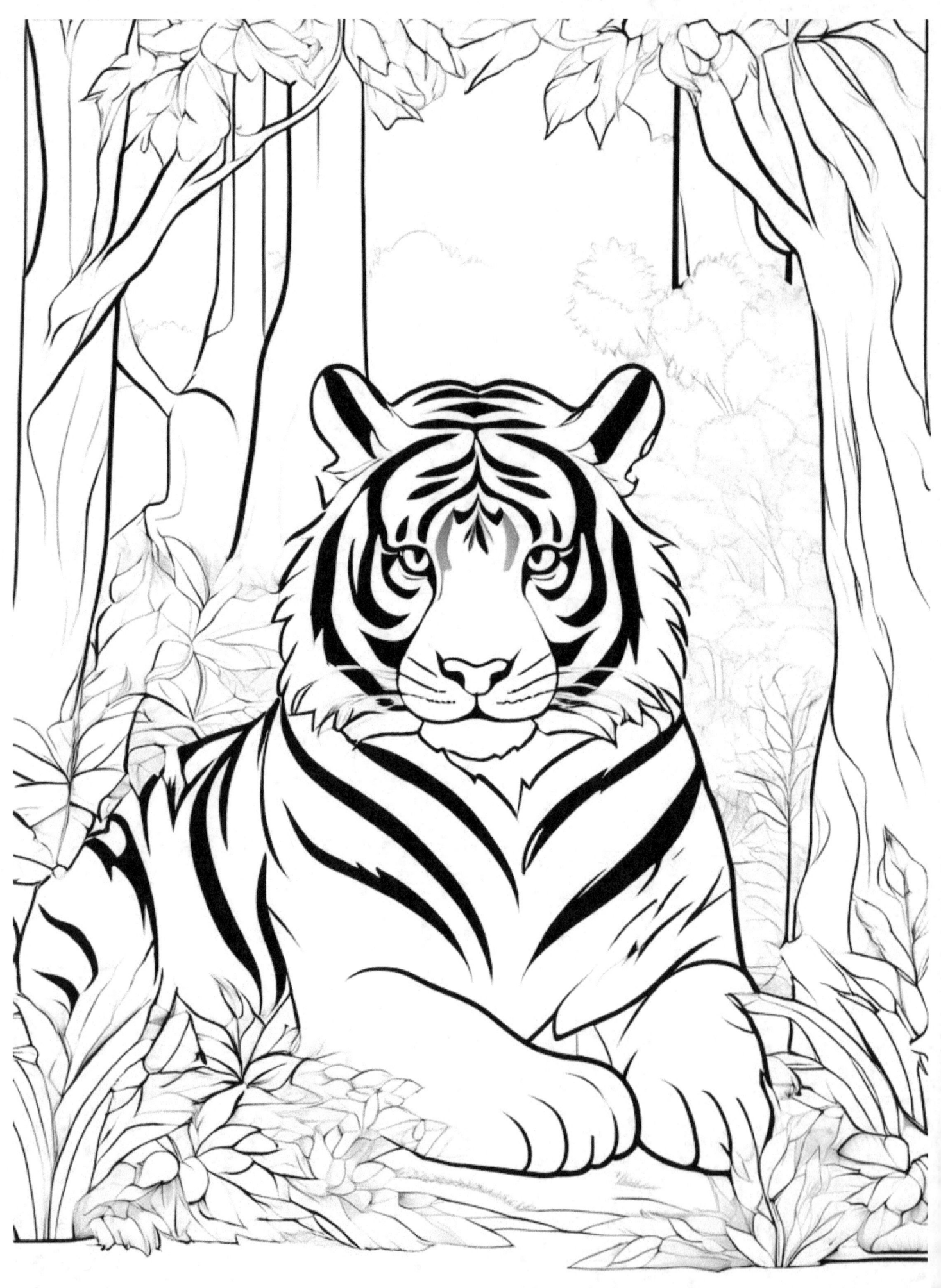

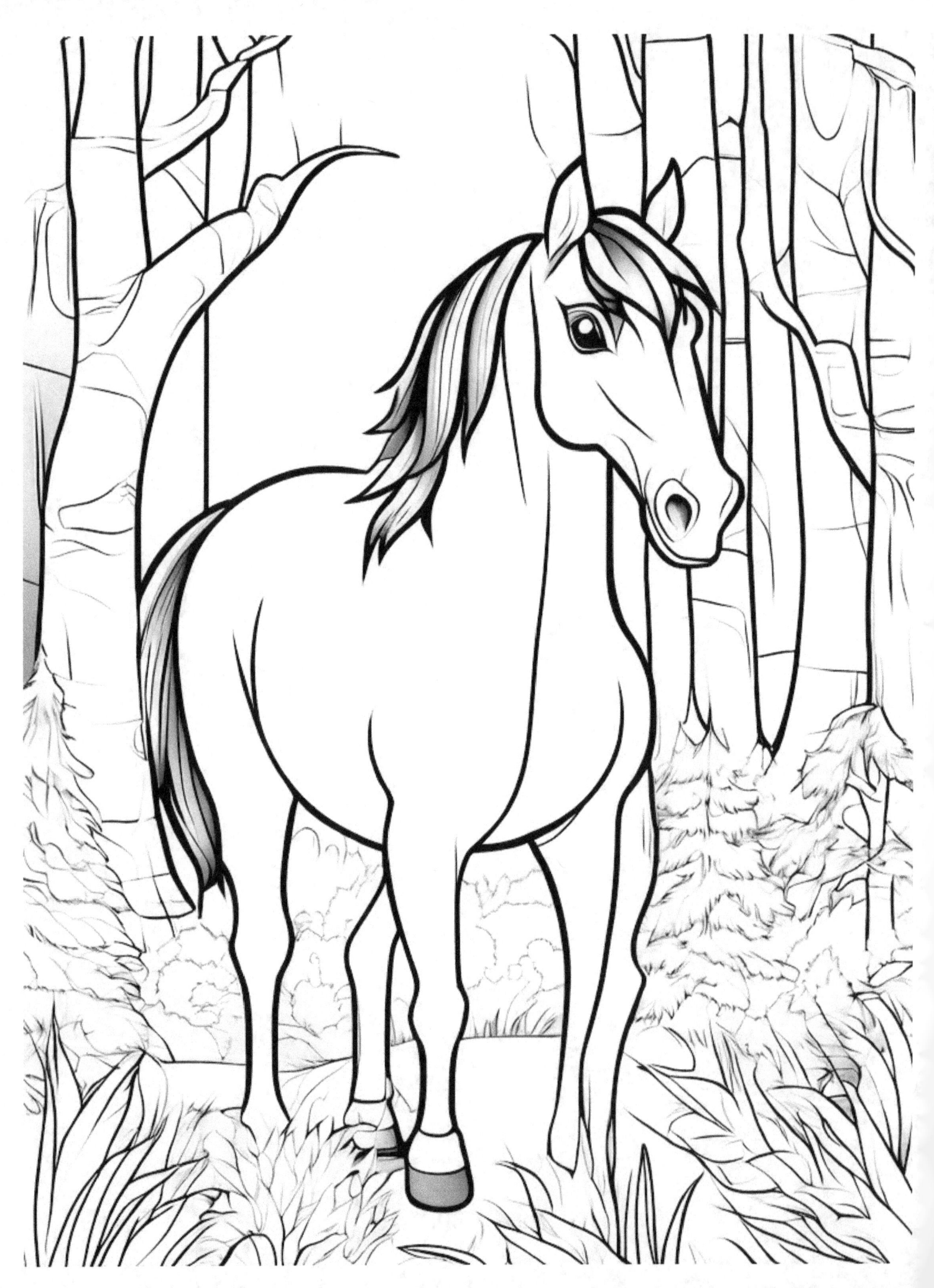

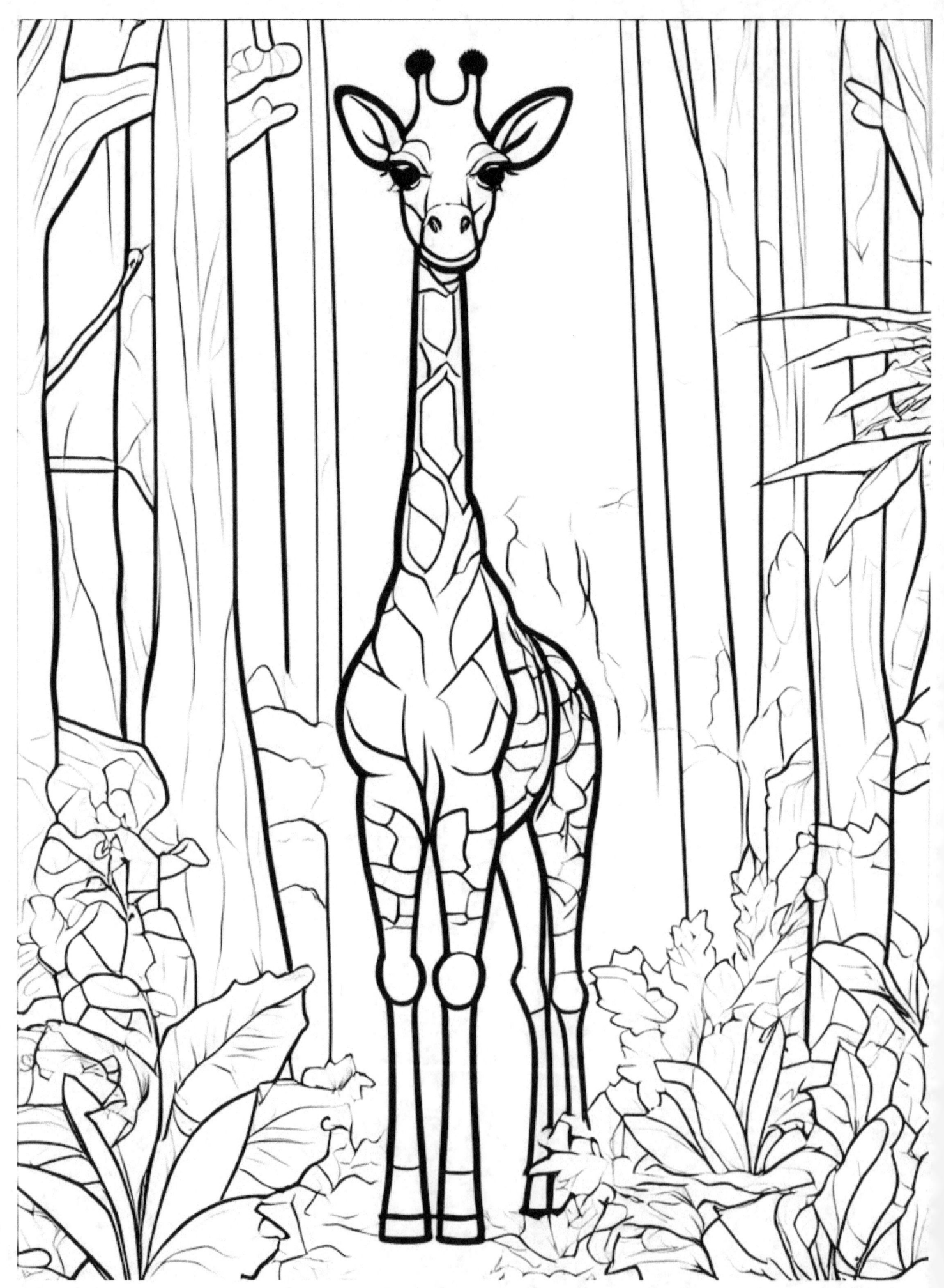

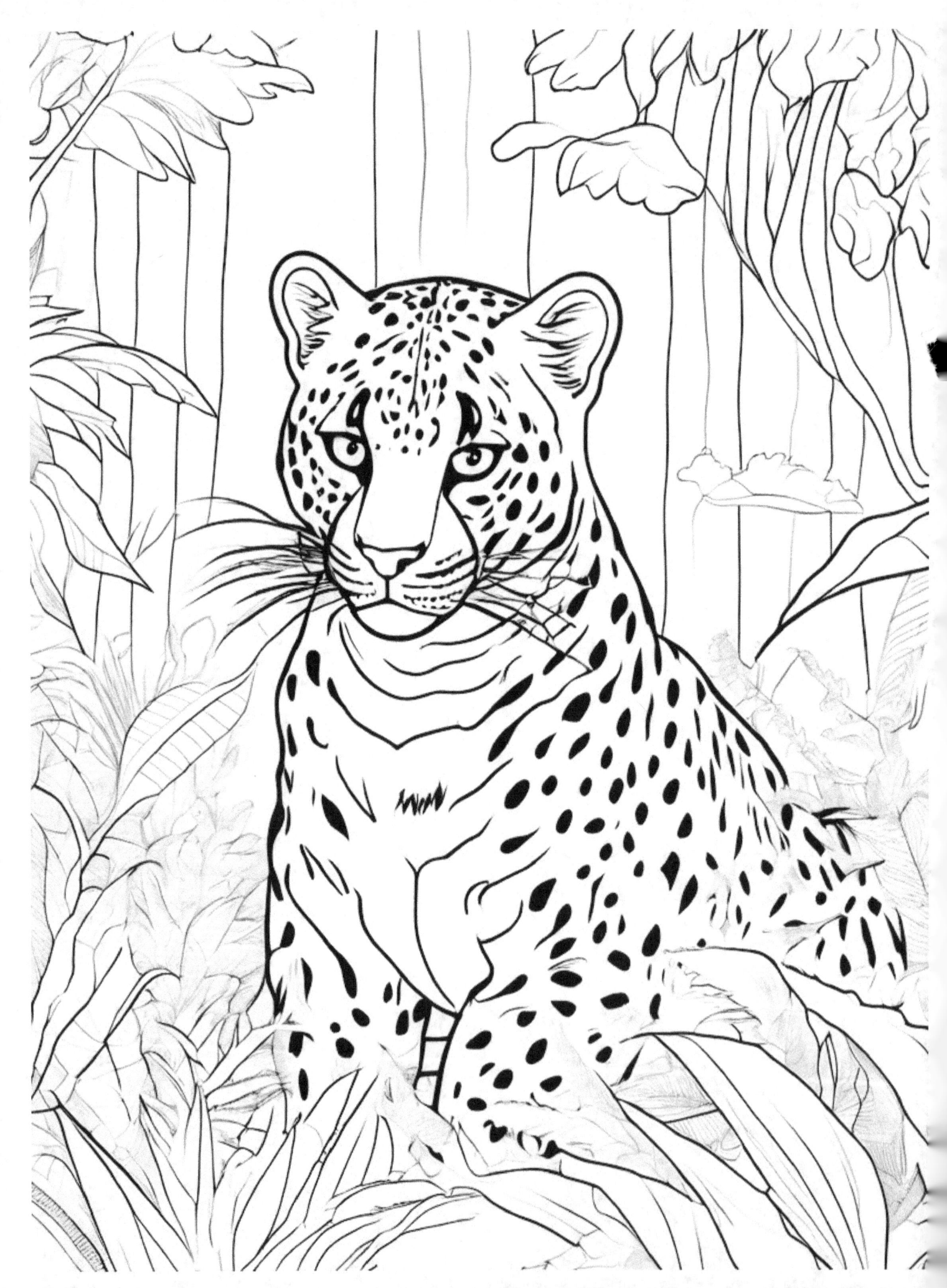